Teen Respect of Self & Others Workbook

Facilitator Reproducible Self-Assessments, Exercises & Educational Handouts

John J. Liptak, EdD
Ester A. Leutenberg

Illustrated by
Amy L. Brodsky, LISW-S

Stress & Wellness Publishers

Duluth, Minnesota

Whole Person
210 West Michigan Street
Duluth, MN 55802-1908

800-247-6789

books@wholeperson.com
www.wholeperson.com

Teen Respect of Self & Others Workbook
Facilitator Reproducible Self-Assessments,
Exercises & Educational Handouts

Copyright ©2011 by Ester A. Leutenberg and John J. Liptak.
All rights reserved. Except for short excerpts for review purposes
and materials in the assessment, journaling activities, and
educational handouts sections, no part of this book may be
reproduced or transmitted in any form by any means, electronic
or mechanical without permission in writing from the publisher.
Self-assessments, exercises, and educational handouts are meant
to be photocopied.

All efforts have been made to ensure accuracy of the information
contained in this book as of the date published. The author(s)
and the publisher expressly disclaim responsibility for any
adverse effects arising from the use or application of the
information contained herein.

Printed in the United States of America

10 9 8 7 6 5 4 3

Editorial Director: Carlene Sippola
Art Director: Joy Morgan Dey

Library of Congress Control Number: 2011927795
ISBN: 978-1-57025-251-8

Using This Book *(For the professional)*

Respect comes in three forms — respect for self, respect for others and respect for community and environment. Although these three forms of respect may not appear to be connected, they are interconnected in several ways:

- For people to show respect to other people, animals, nature, environment and the global community, they must have deep respect for themselves. Without respect for self, it becomes difficult to empathize with the plight of others.
- People are constantly attempting to balance their self-interests and the interests of others.
- A basic human value that individuals strive for is social interest, or the concern and respect for other people in the world and commitment to build a better future for others. Showing social interest and respect is so important that many view it as an indicator of positive mental health and overall wellness. People with little social interest and lack of respect for others tend to be more self-centered and intolerant of others. On the other hand, people who are concerned about others and who want to help others are more likely to have greater life satisfaction, more positive mental health and a greater sense of overall wellness. They are able to develop feelings of happiness and success because they feel pleasure in being respectful and therefore, they experience a sense of social connectedness.

Following is a model that describes the "respecting self and others" cycle of wellness:

By being concerned about others, people experience a greater sense of generosity, contribute to the well-being of others, and find joy in their sense of social interest. This social interest then propels people to be more respectful in the workplace, kinder to the universe, and more apt to be interested in social justice. Whether service to the community (or world) is found through formal organizations or through informal involvement in social issues, people are able to find their own place in the world.

(Continued on the next page)

Using This Book (For the professional, continued)

The *Teen Respect of Self and Others Workbook* contains five separate sections to help participants learn more about themselves, the skills they possess and those they need to learn to be of service to other people and make contributions to the welfare of others. Participants will learn about the importance of these skills in the development of personal and professional success.

The sections of this book are:

1) **SELF-RESPECT SCALE** helps individuals identify their own level of self-respect by exploring their self-confidence, self-efficacy, self-acceptance and self-love.

2) **RESPECT OF OTHERS SCALE** helps individuals identify how respectful they are to other people through their courtesy, caring, tolerance, trust and respect levels.

3) **GENEROSITY SCALE** helps individuals identify and explore their level of generosity with their time, talents and resources.

4) **KINDNESS TO THE GLOBAL COMMUNITY** helps individuals explore how kind and respectful they are in trying to preserve the environment and by focusing on the universe, energy, nature and kind-to-self lifestyle. See Team Suggestion on page 85.

5) **SOCIAL ACTION SCALE** helps individuals identify their altruistic-level and to identify ways to be of service to others in the community by concerning themselves with positive views of others, welfare of others, sense of community and social support.

These sections serve as avenues for individual self-reflection, as well as for group experiences revolving around identified topics of importance. Each assessment includes directions for easy administration, scoring and interpretation. Each section includes exploratory activities, reflective journaling activities and educational handouts to help participants discover their habitual effective and ineffective relationship skills and provides instruction for enhancing their most critical partner-relationship weaknesses.

The art of self-reflection goes back many centuries and is rooted in many of the world's greatest spiritual and philosophical traditions. Socrates, the ancient Greek philosopher, was known to walk the streets engaging the people he met in philosophical reflection and dialogue. He felt that this type of activity was so important in life that he went so far as to proclaim, "The unexamined life is not worth living!" The unexamined life is one in which the same routine is continually repeated without ever thinking about its meaning to one's life and how this life really could be lived. However, a structured reflection and examination of beliefs, assumptions, characteristics, and patterns can provide a better understanding, which can lead to a more satisfying life. A greater level of self-understanding about important life skills is often necessary to make positive, self-directed changes in the negative patterns that keep repeating. The assessments and exercises in this book can help promote this self-understanding. Through involvement in the in-depth activities, the participant claims ownership in the development of positive patterns.

Journaling is an extremely powerful tool for enhancing self-discovery, learning, transcending traditional problems, breaking ineffective life habits, and helping to heal from psychological traumas of the past. From a physical point of view, writing reduces stress and lowers muscle tension, blood pressure and heart rate levels. Psychologically, writing reduces sadness, depression and general anxiety, and leads to a greater level of life satisfaction and optimism. Behaviorally, writing leads to enhanced social skills, emotional intelligence and creativity. It also leads to improved relationship skills which lead to more self-confidence in intimate relationships.

(Continued on the next page)

Using This Book *(For the professional, continued)*

By combining reflective assessment and journaling, participants will be exposed to a powerful method of combining verbalizing and writing to reflect on and solve problems. Participants will become more aware of their outlook in life, the joys and satisfaction they are currently experiencing, and ways of enhancing their life satisfaction.

Preparation for using the assessments and activities in this book is important. The authors suggest that prior to administering any of the assessments in this book, you complete them yourself. This will familiarize you with the format of the assessments, the scoring directions, the interpretation guides and the journaling activities, although the assessments are designed to be self-administered, scored and interpreted. This familiarity will help prepare facilitators to answer questions about the assessments for participants.

About the Assessments, Journaling Activities and Educational Handouts

The Assessments, Journaling Activities, and Educational Handouts in the *Teen Respect of Self and Others Workbook* are reproducible and ready to be photocopied for participants' use. Assessments contained in this book focus on self-reported ideas, beliefs and experiences from the participants. Accuracy and usefulness of the information provided depends on the truthful information that each participant provides through self-examination. By being honest, participants help themselves to learn about unproductive and ineffective friendship patterns, and to uncover information that might be keeping them from being as happy and/or as successful in relationships as they might be.

Advise the teens using the assessments they should not spend too much time trying to analyze the content of the questions; their initial response will most likely be true. Regardless of individual scores, encourage participants to write and talk about their findings and their feelings pertaining to what they have discovered about themselves. Exploring teen respect exercises will be helpful to the teens now and as they mature into adulthood.

USE CODES FOR CONFIDENTIALITY

Confidentiality is a term for any action that preserves the privacy of other people. Because the teens completing the activities in this workbook will be asked to answer assessment items and to journal about people in their lives, you will need to discuss confidentiality before you begin using the materials in this workbook. Maintaining confidentiality is important as it shows respect for others and allows the participants to explore their feelings without hurting anyone's feelings or fearing gossip, harm or retribution.

In order to maintain confidentiality, explain to the participants that they need to assign a code name for each person they write about as they complete the various activities in the workbook. For example, a person they know might have a relative who has blond hair might be titled HBH (Has Blonde Hair) for a particular exercise. In order to protect their identities, they may not use people's actual names or initials – just codes.

Layout of the Book

This Book Includes:

- **Assessment Instruments** – Self-assessment inventories with scoring directions and interpretation materials. Group facilitators can choose one or more of the activities relevant to their participants.
- **Activity Handouts** – Practical questions and activities that prompt self-reflection and promote self-understanding. These questions and activities foster introspection and promote pro-social behaviors.
- **Quotations** – Quotations are used in each section to provide insight and promote self-reflection. Participants will be asked to select one or more of the quotations and journal about what the quotations mean to them.
- **Reflective Questions for Journaling** – Self-exploration activities and journaling exercises specific to each assessment to enhance self-discovery, learning, and healing.
- **Educational Handouts** – Handouts designed to enhance instruction can be used individually or in groups. They can be distributed, converted into masters for overheads or transparencies, projected or written down on a board and discussed.

Who Should Use This Program?

This book has been designed as a practical tool for helping professional therapists, counselors, marriage and family therapists, psychologists, teachers, group leaders, etc. Depending on the role of the professional using the *Teen Respecting Yourself and Others Workbook* and the specific group's needs, these sections can be used individually, combined, or implemented as part of an integrated curriculum for a more comprehensive approach.

Why Use Self-Assessments?

Self-assessments are important in teaching various life skills. Participants will . . .

- Become aware of the primary motivators that guide behavior.
- Explore and learn to indentify potentially harmful situations.
- Explore the effects of messages received in childhood.
- Gain insight that will guide behavioral change.
- Focus their thinking on behavioral goals for change.
- Uncover resources they possess that can help to cope with problems and difficulties.
- Explore their personal characteristics without judgment.
- Develop full awareness of personal strengths and weaknesses.

Because the assessments are presented in a straightforward and easy-to-use format, individuals can self-administer, score and interpret each assessment at their own pace.

Thanks to the following whose input in this book has been so valuable!

Amy L. Brodsky, LISW-S

Carol Butler, MS Ed, RN, C	Kathy Liptak, Ed.D.
Kathy A. Khalsa, MAJS, OTR/L	Eileen Regen, M.Ed., CJE
Jay Leutenberg	Lucy Ritzic, OTR/L

Introduction *(For the participant)*

You often hear that you need to be kind to other people, animals and the universe. Before you can do that, you must be kind to yourself. You need to be yourself and recognize that you are human, find ways to be patient with yourself and forgive yourself. Remember that respect is a two-way street that begins with your ability to respect yourself and then transfer that respect to other people, environment, animals and the global community. To live effectively, you must blend personal motivation and commitment with social commitment and the concern for the well-being and welfare of other people, animals and nature.

Your experiences can have a profound effect on the welfare of others. It can be very easy to respect yourself and work toward your own self-interest; however, respecting and helping others can be a little more challenging. Respecting others suggests it is possible to balance self-interest with respect and concern for others. This workbook is designed to help you look at your level of respect for others and to provide activities to help you to further develop your concern and commitment to others.

Interestingly, all of the research indicates that there are multiple effects when people show respect for others — to the other people, the universe and you. People who help others and show respect and social interest have greater personal and life satisfaction, as well as greater well-being. When you show respect, both you and others will benefit. Social interest has been shown to provide individuals with these feelings:

- purpose and meaning in life
- an inner sense of benevolence
- satisfaction
- pride
- a sense of wellness and decreased stress
- a greater sense of responsibility

You can use this workbook to help you develop the skills and attitudes needed to be more respectful. You will be encouraged throughout the workbook to complete assessments, journaling activities, and exercises. Because active involvement and doing is as important as theories, it is critical that you work hard and take the time to complete all of the skill-building exercises.

IMPORTANT — You will be asked to respond to assessment items and journal about various people in your life. Everyone has the right to confidentiality, and you need to honor the right to privacy of others. Think about it this way — you would not want someone writing things about you that other people could read about. The people in your life feel this way also. Do not use people's actual names when you are listing anyone.

In order to maintain the confidentiality of people you know, assign them code names based on things you know about them. For example, a friend who loves chocolate might have the code of HLC (He Loves Chocolate).

Teen Respect of Self & Others Workbook
TABLE OF CONTENTS

Section I: Self-Respect Scale

    Scale Directions 15
    Scale 16–17
    Scoring Directions 18
    Profile Interpretation 18

Exercises

    Self-Confidence – Stop Comparing Yourself to Others 19
    Self-Confidence – Identify the Cause of
        Your Lack of Self-Confidence 20
    Self-Confidence – Goal Setting 21
    Self-Effectiveness – Actions to Achieving My Goals 22
    Self-Effectiveness – My Competencies 23
    Self-Acceptance – How Others Want Me to Be 24
    Self-Acceptance – What I Like about Myself 25
    Self-Love 26–28
    Self-Love – Accepting Yourself 29–30

Journaling Activities

    Self-Respect Quotations 31

Educational Handouts

    Ways to Respect Yourself 32
    Obstacles to Self-Respect 33

Section II: Respect of Others Scale

    Scale Directions 37
    Scale 38–39
    Scoring Directions 40
    Profile Interpretation 40

Exercises

    Courtesy 41–42
    Care 43–44
    Tolerant 45–46
    Trustworthy 47–48
    Respectful 49–50

TABLE OF CONTENTS

Journaling Activities
    Respect Quotations 51
    Respect - Respectful Examples. 52
    Disrespectful Examples 53–54

Educational Handouts
    How to Build Respect. 55

Section III: Generosity Scale
    Scale Directions 59
    Scale 60
    Scoring Directions 61
    Profile Interpretation 61

Exercises
    Generosity in the Past 62
    Cultivating Generosity 63
    Daily Generosity. 64
    Generosity Motivation 65
    Start Small 66
    Helping Others. 67
    Becoming Dedicated 68
    From Pain Comes Compassion 69
    Being Kind 70–71
    Kindness 72

Journaling Activities
    A Generosity Quotation 73
    Helping 74–76

Educational Handouts
    Facts about Generosity 77

Section IV: Kindness to the Global Community Scale
    Scale Directions 81
    Scale 82–83
    Scoring Directions 84

TABLE OF CONTENTS

    Profile Interpretation 85
    Team Suggestion to the Facilitator. 85

Exercises
    Scale Description – Community – My Social Network 86
    My Past Social Network 87
    My Network. 88
    Scale Description – Energy. 89
    Conserving Energy. 90
    Scale Description – Nature. 91
    Preserving Nature 92
    Scale Description – Kindness to Self Lifestyle. 93
    Defining Success 94
    Redefining Success 95

Journaling Activities
    Kindness to the Global Community Quotations. 96
    Preserving the Global Community 97

Educational Handouts
    Be Kind to the Global Community 98
    Kind People 99

Section V: Social Action Scale

    Scale Directions 103
    Scale 104–105
    Scoring Directions 106
    Profile Interpretation 106
    Descriptions. 107

Exercises
    Reflecting on Your Social Altruism – Motives 108
    Interests. 109
    My Volunteering – Small Projects 110
    My Volunteering – Large Projects 111
    Where or How I Can Help. 112–115
    Benefits of Volunteering. 116
    Why Not? 117

TABLE OF CONTENTS

Journaling Activities
Do Good Anyway.................................118
Being a Volunteer and/or Social Activist 119

Educational Handouts
Excuses People Use to Avoid Helping Others.............120
Tips for Your Volunteer Experiences 121

SECTION I:
Self-Respect Scale

Name_____

Date_____

SECTION I: SELF-RESPECT SCALE

Self Respect Scale Directions

Self-respect is being aware that you are a valuable person and worth being treated with respect and dignity. Self-respect leads to having positive self-esteem and confidence in your unique abilities. The Self-Respect Scale is designed to assess how well you accept and love yourself.

This scale contains 32 statements. Read each of the statements and decide whether or not the statement is true for you. For each of the choices listed, circle the number of your response on the line to the right of each statement.

In the following example, the circled 2 indicates the statement is true for the person completing the assessment:

In most situations . . .

	TRUE	FALSE
I have many talents and positive traits	(2)	1

This is not a test and there are no right or wrong answers. Do not spend too much time thinking about your answers. Your initial response will likely be the most true for you. Be sure to respond to every statement.

(Turn to the next page and begin)

SECTION I: SELF-RESPECT SCALE

Self-Respect Scale

In most situations . . .

	TRUE	FALSE
I have many talents and positive traits	2	1
I worry about how others view me	1	2
I have good common sense	2	1
I tend to be a perfectionist	1	2
I believe I can accomplish what I set out to do	2	1
I have a hard time overcoming obstacles and challenges	1	2
I have good judgment	2	1
I rarely push myself beyond my physical and mental limits	1	2

SC - TOTAL = _____

In most situations . . .

	TRUE	FALSE
I know I can achieve my goals	2	1
I am able to influence events in my life	2	1
I do well in a learning environment	2	1
I have a hard time mastering new things	1	2
I am confident I will do well in anything I want to do	2	1
I am able to perform at high levels most of the time	2	1
I sometimes have a hard time learning	1	2
I give up easily	1	2

SE - TOTAL = _____

(Continued on the next page)

SECTION I: SELF-RESPECT SCALE

(Self-Respect Scale continued)

In most situations . . .

	TRUE	FALSE
I feel free to be myself	2	1
I am okay just the way I am	2	1
I have trouble accepting my weaknesses	1	2
I often act differently to be one of the crowd	1	2
I always try to improve	2	1
I often do not respect myself	1	2
I do not concern myself as to how others view me	2	1
I often feel misunderstood	1	2

SA - TOTAL = _____

In most situations . . .

	TRUE	FALSE
I love who I am right now	2	1
I realize that I am constantly changing and growing	2	1
I do not always like myself	1	2
I focus on my strengths, not my weaknesses	2	1
I have value as a human being, just as I am	2	1
I love the ways I am unique from other people	2	1
I would rather be someone else	1	2
I am a worthwhile person	2	1

SL - TOTAL = _____

(Go to the Scoring Directions on the next page)

SECTION I: SELF-RESPECT SCALE

Self-Respect Scale Scoring Directions

In order for you to respect others, you need to first respect yourself. Too often people try to live up to the expectations of others while repressing their own sense of self-respect. For each of the four sections on the previous pages, add the scores you circled. Put each total on the line marked TOTAL at the end of each section.

Then, transfer your totals to the spaces below:

SC - SELF-CONFIDENCE TOTAL = _____

SE - SELF-EFFECTIVENESS TOTAL = _____

SA - SELF-ACCEPTANCE = _____

SL - SELF-LOVE TOTAL = _____

Add the section totals for your **GRAND TOTAL** = _____

Profile Interpretation

Total Scale Scores	Grand Total Scores	Result	Indications
14 to 16	54 to 64	high	You have developed many of the attitudes, beliefs, and values that are necessary to have and to maintain a positive sense of self-respect. The exercises that follow will help you to grow even further.
11 to 13	42 to 53	moderate	You have developed some of the attitudes, beliefs, and values that are necessary to have and to maintain a positive sense of self-respect. The exercises that follow will help you be even more respectful to yourself.
8 to 10	32 to 41	low	You have not yet developed many of the attitudes, beliefs, and values that are necessary to have and to maintain a positive sense of self-respect. The exercises that follow will help you to enhance your self-respect.

For scales on which you scored in the **Moderate** or **Low** range, find corresponding exercises on the pages that follow. Read the descriptions and complete the exercises that are included. No matter how you scored, low, moderate or high, you will benefit from these exercises.

SECTION I: ACTIVITY HANDOUTS

Self-Confidence

People scoring high on the self-confidence scale are self-assured and accepting of their abilities, behaviors, physical appearance and other characteristics.

Stop Comparing Yourself to Others

When you compare yourself to others, you will always find something that you like better in other people. In the table that follows, list the codes of some of the people with whom you tend to compare yourself and what you like better about these people than yourself. Use name code, not initials. (HRH = Has Red Hair)

People I Compare Myself With (use name code)	What I like Better About Them than Myself

SECTION I: ACTIVITY HANDOUTS

Identify the Cause of Your Lack of Self-Confidence

It is important to identify where and why you feel a lack of self-confidence. In the table below, identify some of the reasons you feel vulnerable or not as good as other people.

	Reasons I Feel Self-Confident	Reasons I Lack Self-Confidence
My Physical Appearance		
My Cultural, Religious, Spiritual, Ethic, Sexual and/or Gender Differences		
My Brain Power		
My School Success		
My Past		
My Family		
My Friends		
My Talents		
Other		

SECTION I: ACTIVITY HANDOUTS

Self-Confidence Goal Setting

Setting goals can boost your self-confidence. In the table below, set some personal, school and/or work-related goals that you might like to achieve within the next year.

Type of Goal	Personal Goals	School and/or Work Goals
Short-range goals (those you would like to accomplish in the next 3 months)	*(Ex: read 2 books, non-school related)*	*(Ex: get a part time job)*
Medium-range goals (those you would like to accomplish in the next 6 months)	*(Ex: volunteer at the hunger center)*	*(Ex: get better grades)*
Long-range goals (those you would like to accomplish in the next year)	*Ex: travel to see my cousin)*	*(Ex: learn a second language)*

SECTION I: ACTIVITY HANDOUTS

Self-Effectiveness – Actions to Achieve My Goals

People scoring high on the self-effectiveness scale believe they have the ability to perform well and meet their personal and professional goals.

Setting goals can boost your self-confidence. In the spaces below, identify the tasks that you will accomplish to meet your personal and professional (school and job related) goals.

Type of Goal	How I Will Begin to Achieve My Personal Goals	How I Will Begin to Achieve School and/or Work Goals
Short-range goals (those you would like to accomplish in the next 3 months)	(Ex: ask others about their favorite books)	(Ex: check out the want ads in the newspaper and online for job opportunities)
Medium-range goals (those you would like to accomplish in the next 6 months)	(Ex: check my schedule and decide how much time I have and when)	(Ex: improve my study habits)
Long-range goals (those you would like to accomplish in the next year)	(Ex: put money in a savings account for my trip)	(Ex: investigate library and community college for opportunity)

SECTION I: ACTIVITY HANDOUTS

Self-Effectiveness – My Competencies

In the table that follows, list your talents, skills and abilities – things you are good at. These can be competencies you learned at home, in school, on a job, volunteering, from people who influenced you or those you have acquired on your own.

Things I am Good at	What Makes Me So Good
(Ex: I listen to my friends' problems.)	*(Ex: I listen carefully, have good eye contact, don't interrupt or judge them, and keep their confidence.)*

Self-Acceptance – How Others Want Me to Be

People scoring high on the self-acceptance scale accept themselves for who they are as human beings, despite their weaknesses. It is important that you accept yourself for who you are and that you don't try to live up to other people's views of how you should be. Below, identify how you think others want you to be, and describe how you really are.

How Others Want Me to Be	How I Am
(Ex: My friends want me to be with them, or communicating with them constantly.)	Ex: I like spending time with my family, especially my aging grandmother.)

SECTION I: ACTIVITY HANDOUTS

Self-Acceptance – What I Like About Myself

We all have things we like about ourselves. In the spaces that follow, describe some of the things you like about yourself.

Things to Like	What I like About Myself
My appearance	
My values	
My relationships	
My accomplishments	
My personality	
My talents	
Other	
Other	
Other	

SECTION I: ACTIVITY HANDOUTS

Self-Love

People scoring high on the self-love scale tend to love themselves unconditionally.

What do you love about yourself?
_____
_____
_____
_____
_____

What do other people love about you?
_____
_____
_____
_____
_____

How can you better honor who you are?
_____
_____
_____
_____
_____

In what ways are you growing as a person?
_____
_____
_____
_____
_____

(Continued on the next page)

SECTION I: ACTIVITY HANDOUTS

Self-Love *(Continued)*

What kind of a person would you like to be in five years?

___

What are your strengths?

___

How can you better celebrate these strengths?

___

How are you unique?

___

Do you have a lack of self-love in any areas of your life? What are they?

___

(Continued on the next page)

Self-Love (Continued)

What do you believe is causing any lack of self-love you might have?

_____
_____
_____
_____

What aspect of yourself would you praise?

_____
_____
_____
_____

What types of self-critical messages do you send yourself?

_____
_____
_____
_____

What self-talk can you say to those self-critical messages?

_____
_____
_____
_____

How do you love and nurture yourself?

_____
_____
_____
_____

SECTION I: ACTIVITY HANDOUTS

Self-Love – Accepting Yourself

What do you like and accept most about yourself?

_____
_____
_____
_____
_____
_____

What do you like and accept about yourself that others may not?

_____
_____
_____
_____
_____
_____

Do you feel a need to make a change? If so, why? How?

_____
_____
_____
_____
_____
_____

Do you think you will change some day? When?

_____
_____
_____
_____
_____
_____

(Continued on the next page)

SECTION I: ACTIVITY HANDOUTS

Accepting Yourself *(Continued)*

What is most difficult for you to accept about yourself?

_____
_____
_____
_____

Is it something you could change?

_____
_____
_____
_____

If you can change it, how will you start to make the change?

_____
_____
_____
_____

If you cannot change it, how can you be more accepting about it?

_____
_____
_____
_____

Whom can you talk to about it?

_____
_____
_____
_____

SECTION I: JOURNALING ACTIVITIES

Self-Respect Quotations

Choose two of the quotes below. How does each speak to your feelings about self-respect? Perhaps you will find a quote that you disagree with. Write about it also.

- *The willingness to accept responsibility for one's own life is the source from which self-respect springs.* ~ **Joan Didion**

- *Self-respect permeates every aspect of your life.* ~ **Joe Clark**

- *Respect yourself and others will respect you.* ~ **Confucius**

- *Self-respect cannot be hunted. It cannot be purchased. It is never for sale. It cannot be fabricated out of public relations. It comes to us when we are alone, in quiet moments, in quiet places, when we suddenly realize that, knowing the good, we have done it; knowing the beautiful, we have served it; knowing the truth we have spoken it.* ~ **Whitney Griswold**

Ways to Respect Myself

- Respect others
- Hang out with positive people
- Use positive self-talk when you are being critical of yourself
- Eliminate self-minimizing phrases:

    "I shoulda"

    "I coulda"

    "I woulda"
- Feel your own feelings, not others'
- Take appropriate risks
- Choose like-minded friends
- Know you are OK, even if you are not perfect
- Set achievable goals
- Celebrate your strengths
- Do your own thing because you want to, not because you're keeping up with others

Obstacles to Self-Respect

- Fear of healthy risk-taking
- Insecurity
- Fear of failure
- Disliking yourself
- Fear of rejection by others
- Perfectionist thinking
- Need for approval
- Disliking your actions
- Fear of establishing close relationships
- Dwelling on the past
- Irrational thinking
- Feeling compelled to keep up with others, no matter what

SECTION II:
Respect of Others Scale

Name_____

Date_____

SECTION II: ENVIRONMENTAL AGGRESSION SCALE

Respect of Others Scale Directions

One of the most important traits one can have is being respectful of others.

Respect includes these aspects:
- a positive feeling about someone or something
- an attitude in which you treat others the way you would like to be treated
- value of others' beliefs, ideas, feelings and actions
- courtesy, caring, tolerance, respectfulness and trustworthiness

This assessment will help you identify your level of respect of others. Read each statement carefully. Circle the number of the response that shows how descriptive each statement is of you.

Please respond to each of the statements by circling the response which best describes you:

4 = Always   3 = Often   2 = Sometimes   1 = Rarely, if Ever

1. I say please and thank you to people. 4   3   ②   1

In the above example, the circled 2 indicates that the person taking the scale sometimes says please and thank you to people.

This is not a test and there are no right or wrong answers. Do not spend too much time thinking about your answers. Your initial response will likely be the most true for you. Be sure to respond to every statement.

(Turn to the next page and begin)

© 2011 WHOLE PERSON ASSOCIATES, 210 WEST MICHIGAN ST., DULUTH MN 55802-1908 ▪ 800-247-6789

SECTION I: RESPECT OF OTHERS SCALE

Respect of Others Scale

Please respond to each of the statements by circling the response which best describes you:

4 = Always   3 = Often   2 = Sometimes   1 = Rarely, if Ever

1. I say please and thank you to people.	4	3	2	1
2. I show courtesy to adults with my spoken and body language.	4	3	2	1
3. I am interested in others, not just myself.	4	3	2	1
4. I look people in the eye when talking to them.	4	3	2	1
5. I am kind to the people I live with.	4	3	2	1
6. I am gentle, not forceful, both emotionally and physically.	4	3	2	1
7. I speak nicely to people, even if I don't know them.	4	3	2	1

I = _____

8. I express gratitude to the people in my life.	4	3	2	1
9. I think about how my actions affect others.	4	3	2	1
10. I am compassionate.	4	3	2	1
11. I am sensitive to other people's feelings.	4	3	2	1
12. I am not a mean or hurtful person.	4	3	2	1
13. I forgive easily and don't hold a grudge.	4	3	2	1
14. I do caring things for people in need.	4	3	2	1

II = _____

15. I am accepting of all people who are different from me in any way.	4	3	2	1
16. I do not feel or act superior to other people.	4	3	2	1
17. I do not have a chip on my shoulder.	4	3	2	1
18. I think other people are authentic, unless they prove otherwise.	4	3	2	1
19. I do not get offended easily.	4	3	2	1
20. I am open-minded.	4	3	2	1
21. I am patient with my family members.	4	3	2	1

III = _____

(Continued on the next page)

SECTION II: RESPECT OF OTHERS SCALE

(Respect of Others Scale continued)

Please respond to each of the statements by circling the response which best describes you:

4 = Always   3 = Often   2 = Sometimes   1 = Rarely, if Ever

22. I want to be worthy of people's respect for me	4	3	2	1
23. I have the courage to do the right thing, even if it is not popular	4	3	2	1
24. I have no problem keeping my promises	4	3	2	1
25. I always do what I say I will do	4	3	2	1
26. I show character even if no one is watching	4	3	2	1
27. People say I can be counted on	4	3	2	1
28. My family can depend on me	4	3	2	1

IV = _____

29. I am not judgmental of other people or their viewpoints	4	3	2	1
30. I treat others the way I like to be treated	4	3	2	1
31. I am able to apologize when I am wrong	4	3	2	1
32. I handle problems thoughtfully and peacefully	4	3	2	1
33. I am considerate of others' feelings	4	3	2	1
34. I respect other people's belongings and property	4	3	2	1
35. I make sure my friends value my family and home	4	3	2	1

V = _____

(Go to the Scoring Directions on the next page)

SECTION II: RESPECT OF OTHERS SCALE

Respect of Others Scale
Scoring Directions

The scale you just completed will help you identify your respect level. Add the scores you circled for each of the sections. Put each total on the line marked TOTAL at the end of each section. Transfer your totals to the spaces below, and then add them for a GRAND TOTAL.

TOTALS

I. _____ **Courteous Scale:** Behaves in a polite and courteous manner

II. _____ **Caring Scale:** Shows kindness, compassion and respect to others

III. _____ **Tolerant Scale:** Accepts different views and actions

IV. _____ **Trustworthy Scale:** Impress others with integrity

V. _____ **Respectful Scale:** Feels acceptance, admiration and respect for others

_____ **GRAND TOTAL**

After transferring your scores, review the Profile Interpretations below for more information about your scores.

Profile Interpretation

Total Individual Scale Scores	Grand Total Scores	Result	Indications
22 to 28	103 to 140	high	You tend to be a very respectful person. Continue to be as respectful as possible.
14 to 21	65 to 102	moderate	You tend to be a somewhat respectful person. Continue to be respectful and complete the exercises and activities to become even more respectful.
7 to 13	28 to 64	low	You are probably not as respectful as you could be. The exercises and activities will help you to become more respectful.

Complete the exercises included in this scale. Whether you scored, low, moderate or high, you will benefit from these exercises.

SECTION II: ACTIVITY HANDOUTS

Courtesy

To whom do you feel you are courteous?

Think about people in your life and identify ways in which you are courteous.

Use a name code for each person but not initials. (IACL = Is A Cheer Leader)

People in My Life	How I Am Courteous to Them
Ex: Family members	Ex: When JLM shops I bring in the bags and help to put the groceries away.
Family members	
Friends	
Co-Workers	
Neighbors	
People in my community	
Supervisors/Teachers	
Other	

© 2011 WHOLE PERSON ASSOCIATES, 210 WEST MICHIGAN ST., DULUTH MN 55802-1908 ▪ 800-247-6789

SECTION II: ACTIVITY HANDOUTS

Courtesy (Continued)

Now think about people in your life and identify ways in which you are not courteous to them and how you can be more courteous to them in the future.

Use a name code for each person but not initials.

People in My Life	How I Am Not Courteous	How I Will Be More Courteous
Ex: Family members	Ex: When MBB struggles with his homework, I am too busy to help.	Ex: I will help him with homework more often.
Family members		
Friends		
Co-Workers		
Neighbors		
People in my community		
Supervisors/ Teachers		
Other		

SECTION II: ACTIVITY HANDOUTS

Care

Who do you care about?

Think about people in your life and identify ways in which you show them you care.

Use a name code for each person but not initials.

People in My Life	How I Show That I Care
Ex: Family members	*Ex: I go over to GMA's house and read to her.*
Family members	
Friends	
Co-Workers	
Neighbors	
People in my community	
Supervisors / Teachers	
Other	

SECTION II: ACTIVITY HANDOUTS

Care (Continued)

Now think about people in your life and identify ways in which you do not show them that you care. Think about how you can be more caring in the future.

Use a name code for each person but not initials.

People in My Life	How I DO NOT Show That I Care	How I WILL Show That I Care
Ex: Family members	Ex: I always forget family birthdays!	Ex: I will set up a calendar on my computer.
Family members		
Friends		
Co-Workers		
Neighbors		
People in my community		
Supervisors / Teachers		
Other		

SECTION II: ACTIVITY HANDOUTS

Tolerant

To whom do you feel you show tolerance?
Think about people in your life and identify ways in which you show tolerance.

Use a name code for each person but not initials.

People in My Life	How I Am Tolerant of Them
Ex: Family members	Ex: I am patient with QRA when he asks me to do the same thing every day.
Family members	
Friends	
Co-Workers	
Neighbors	
People in my community	
Supervisors/ Teachers	
Other	

SECTION II: ACTIVITY HANDOUTS

Tolerant *(Continued)*

Now think about people in your life and identify ways in which you are not tolerant of them and how you can be more tolerant of them in the future.

Use a name code for each person but not initials.

People in My Life	How I Am Not Tolerant	How I Will Be More Tolerant
Ex: Family members	Ex: I get angry when constantly being told to be careful.	Ex: I will explain that I will be careful without being reminded and will try to understand that she worries.
Family members		
Friends		
Co-Workers		
Neighbors		
People in my community		
Supervisors/ Teachers		
Other		

SECTION II: ACTIVITY HANDOUTS

Trustworthy

Who feels you are trustworthy? Think about people in your life and identify ways in which you demonstrate your trustworthiness.

Use a name code for each person but not initials.

People in My Life	How I Am Trustworthy
Ex: Family members	*Ex: I have never lied to AAL and for that reason she believes whatever I say.*
Family members	
Friends	
Co-Workers	
Neighbors	
People in my community	
Supervisors/ Teachers	
Other	

SECTION II: ACTIVITY HANDOUTS

Trustworthy *(Continued)*

Now think about people in your life again and identify ways in which you are not seen as trustworthy. Think about how you can be more trustworthy in the future.

Use a name code for each person but not initials.

People in My Life	How I Am Not Trustworthy	How I Will Be More Trustworthy
Ex: Family members	Ex: I say I'll be home at a certain time and I am usually late.	Ex: I can tell HDE that I am going to start being on time and then set my cell phone alarm to remind myself.
Family members		
Friends		
Co-Workers		
Neighbors		
People in my community		
Supervisors/ Teachers		
Other		

SECTION II: ACTIVITY HANDOUTS

Respectful

To whom do you feel you are respectful? Think about people in your life and identify ways in which you demonstrate your respectfulness.

Use a name code for each person but not initials.

People in My Life	How I Am Respectful of Them
Ex: Family members	*Ex: I respect MZ so very much. I call him every week and I send him papers that I write that I think will be of interest to him.*
Family members	
Friends	
Co-Workers	
Neighbors	
People in my community	
Supervisors/ Teachers	
Other	

SECTION II: ACTIVITY HANDOUTS

Respectful *(Continued)*

Now think about people in your life again and identify ways in which you are not respectful to them and how you can be more respectful in the future.

Use a name code for each person but not initials.

People in My Life	How I Am Not Respectful	How I Will Be More Respectful
Ex: Family members	Ex: I get upset with UBG and I roll my eyes, slam doors, and am very grumpy.	Ex: I need to remember how much UBG loves me and try responding in a more positive way.
Family members		
Friends		
Co-Workers		
Neighbors		
People in my community		
Supervisors / Teachers		
Other		

SECTION II: JOURNALING AVTIVITIES

Respect Quotations

Put check marks by the quotes that you feel might inspire you to integrate respect as an important value in your life. You can cut the quotes out and post them by your computer, on your refrigerator, or tuck them into your wallet. At the bottom of the page, write about why those particular quotes speak to you.

❏ *Be modest, be respectful of others, try to understand.* ~ **Lakhdar Brahimi**

❏ *Too often we underestimate the power of a touch, a smile, a kind word, a listening ear, and honest compliment, or the smallest act of caring, all of which have the potential to turn a life around.* ~ **Leo F. Buscaglia**

❏ *The best thing to give to your enemy is forgiveness; to an opponent, tolerance; to a friend, your heart; to your child, a good example; to a father, deference; to your mother, conduct that will make her proud of you; to yourself, respect; to all people, charity.* ~ **Benjamin Franklin**

❏ *No one is too big to be courteous, but some are too little.* ~ **Anonymous**

❏ *You may be deceived if you trust too much, but you will live in torment if you do not trust enough.* ~ **Frank Crane**

_____
_____
_____
_____
_____
_____
_____
_____
_____
_____
_____
_____

SECTION II: JOURNALING ACTIVITIES

Respect

How do you define respect? _____
_____
_____
_____

Respectful Examples

Choose two actions below, and give an example of how each of these terms could indicate respect. You can use an actual experience (if you are referring to someone else, use a code) or you can use your imagination to make up a scenario involving that word.

Honor _____
_____
_____
_____

Show regard _____
_____
_____
_____

Display esteem _____
_____
_____
_____

Act in a considerate way _____
_____
_____
_____

SECTION II: JOURNALING ACTIVITIES

Disrespectful Examples

Choose two words below, and give an example of how each of these terms could involve disrespect. You can use an actual experience (if you are referring to someone else, use a code) or you can use your imagination to make up a scenario involving that word.

Rudeness _____
_____
_____
_____
_____
_____

Discourtesy _____
_____
_____
_____
_____
_____

Insult _____
_____
_____
_____
_____
_____

Ridicule _____
_____
_____
_____
_____
_____

(Continued on the next page)

SECTION II: JOURNALING ACTIVITIES

Disrespectful Examples *(Continued)*

Bad Manners _____
_____
_____
_____
_____
_____

Aggression _____
_____
_____
_____
_____
_____

Profanity _____
_____
_____
_____
_____
_____

Humiliation _____
_____
_____
_____
_____
_____

How to Build Respect

- Treat others as you expect them to treat you
- Enjoy the traditions and cultures of others
- Regard authority
- Speak kindly about others
- Honor limits and boundaries
- Accept others' differences
- Never stop learning
- Avoid gossip
- Recognize others' accomplishments
- Respect when someone says, "No"
- Do not give up
- Be responsible
- Maintain a positive attitude
- Admit when you are wrong
- Avoid embarrassing yourself or others. Remember courtesy, caring, tolerance, respect and trust

SECTION III:
Generosity Scale

Name_____

Date_____

SECTION III: GENEROSITY SCALE

Generosity Scale Directions

GENEROSITY IS . . .

- giving of your time, energy, talents, and resources to help other people
- helping others without expecting anything in return
- moving from self-interest to the social interest of other people

This assessment contains 35 statements related to the acts of caring and giving to other people. Read each of the statements and decide whether or not the statement describes you. If the statement does describe you, circle the number under the YES column next to that item. If the statement does not describe you, circle the number under the NO column next to that item.

In the following example, the circled number under YES indicates the person completing this scale does not care about the happiness of others.

	YES	NO
I don't care about the happiness of others	(1)	2

This is not a test and there are no right or wrong answers. Do not spend too much time thinking about your answers. Your initial response will likely be the most true for you. Be sure to respond to every statement.

(Turn to the next page and begin)

SECTION III: GENEROSITY SCALE

Generosity Scale

	YES	NO
I don't care about the happiness of others	1	2
I like to share what I have with others	2	1
Helping others is rewarding for me	2	1
I am not motivated to help others	1	2
I like to be charitable anonymously	2	1
I help people less fortunate than me	2	1
I give to others out of guilt	1	2
I feel good about myself when I help others	2	1
I only give to others because I can't say no	1	2
Giving is a spiritual practice for me	2	1
I feel dedicated to a higher goal in life	2	1
I learn and grow from helping others	2	1
Others say I am selfish	1	2
I often do good works, but I do them quietly	2	1
I give to others, but I expect something in return	1	2
I am concerned about the welfare of the world	2	1
I am always trying to work toward a higher purpose	2	1
I feel loving when I help others	2	1
I expect recognition for helping others	1	2
I often volunteer to help others	2	1
I see no need to help others	1	2
I like to share my time and energy with others	2	1
I expect rewards when I help others	1	2
I enjoy being charitable	2	1
I am too busy to help others	1	2
I enjoy the act of giving more than the thanks I receive	2	1
I can empathize with people who are suffering	2	1
I feel bad when people don't have their basic needs met	2	1
I am not dedicated to a purpose higher than my own satisfaction	1	2
I look for ways to serve all living creatures	2	1
I am compassionate towards other people	2	1
I don't know, or care, what I can to do help others	1	2
I enjoy giving small gifts to others	2	1
I like to share what I have with others	2	1
I don't feel appreciated when I do things for others	1	2

TOTAL _____

(Go to the Scoring Directions on the next page)

SECTION III: GENEROSITY SCALE

Generosity Scale Scoring Directions

This scale is designed to help you explore your generosity toward others. Add the numbers that you circled on the previous page and place it in the TOTAL line. Put your score in the space below.

GENEROSITY TOTAL = _____

There are three stages in the cultivation of generosity. See below to interpret your scores and identify which stage you are currently in.

Profile Interpretation

Total Scale Scores	Result	Indications
59 to 70	high	Generosity is highly developed for you. You give effortlessly and spontaneously, and you naturally want to give the best of what is yours to maximize the happiness of others. The welfare of other people is as important as your own, and your happiness increases when other people are happy. At this stage it is clear that serving people is a privilege and a joy for you.
47 to 58	moderate	You offer gifts and give willingly, happy to share your blessings with other people. You are motivated by your well-being and that of other people.
35 to 46	low	You offer gifts hesitantly. You fear that you might want or need those items later. You don't concern yourself with others' problems. You are more concerned with your own fears than other people's needs.

Generosity toward others and the desire to help people in need is a life quality that can be cultivated. Regardless of your scores on the assessment you just completed, the following exercises are designed to help you learn ways to either begin or continue to develop your generosity.

SECTION III: ACTIVITY HANDOUTS

Generosity in the Past

Before you begin to cultivate generosity, it is important to look at how you have been generous in the past. In the spaces that follow, write about the ways you have been generous to people, organizations, charities, etc. in your life.

For each person, organization, or charity you mention, use a name code but not initials.

People, Organization, Charity in My Life	How I Have Been Generous

SECTION III: ACTIVITY HANDOUTS

Cultivating Generosity

It is important to think about how you would like to help others. At this point don't worry about what you think you should do, but think about what you would like to do. In the spaces that follow, list some of the talents and gifts you possess that you could share with others. Then think about where you might want to offer your special talents. Be creative and identify potential sources of people who could benefit from your talents.

For each person you mention, use a name code but not initials.

Talents and/or Gifts I Possess	How I Can Use These Talents and/or Gifts	Where I Can Use These Talents and/or Gifts
Ex: I'm great with computers.	Ex: I could teach people who don't know how to use a computer.	Ex: I can volunteer at the local senior center in my town.

© 2011 WHOLE PERSON ASSOCIATES, 210 WEST MICHIGAN ST., DULUTH MN 55802-1908 • 800-247-6789

SECTION III: ACTIVITY HANDOUTS

Daily Generosity

Generosity does not always pertain to working through a formal organization. Think about ways that you can be more kind and generous to the people in your life. Below, list the people in your life and how you might be more kind and/or generous to them.

For each person you mention, use a name code but not initials.

People in My Life	How I Will be More Generous
Family Members	
Special Friends	
School Acquaintances	
Teachers and School Personnel	
Neighbors	
Community Residents	
Co-Workers	
Others	

SECTION III: ACTIVITY HANDOUTS

Generosity Motivation

It is important to reflect on your motivation for being generous to others. Answer the following questions about your motivations for wanting to help others.

For each person you mention, use a name code but not initials.

In your opinion, what does one derive from being generous to other people?

_____
_____
_____
_____

How can selfishness, greed and jealousy interfere with one's desire to help others?

_____
_____
_____
_____

What gratifications do you feel when you serve others?

_____
_____
_____
_____

How can you make giving a more enjoyable process?

_____
_____
_____
_____

How can you be generous without spending money?

_____
_____
_____
_____

SECTION III: ACTIVITY HANDOUTS

Start Small

It is important to begin being generous in small ways. How can you begin giving by starting small? Answer the following questions to begin your journey to generosity.

For each person you mention, use a name code but not initials.

What small gifts or services could you give to your family members?

_____
_____
_____
_____

What small gifts or services could you give to your friends?

_____
_____
_____
_____

What small gifts or services could you give to new people in the neighborhood?

_____
_____
_____
_____

What small gifts or services could you give to your co-workers?

_____
_____
_____
_____

What small gifts or services could you give to a senior citizen center?

_____
_____
_____
_____

SECTION III: ACTIVITY HANDOUTS

Helping Others

Think about paid or volunteer work in which you have participated. This might include part or full-time jobs, chores, volunteering, babysitting, or helping family and friends. Regardless of the type of volunteering or work you are doing, or have done, it is helping others.

For each person you mention, use a name code but not initials.

Who do you help?
 (Ex: I help to take care of GMJ.)

_____
_____
_____

How do you do this?
 (Ex: I come to her house 3 times a week and help her.)

_____
_____
_____

What steps can you take to enhance the service you provide?
 (Ex: I can be more cheerful.)

_____
_____
_____

How can this be turned into a pleasant experience for yourself, too?
 (Ex: Bring a funny DVD.)

_____
_____
_____

How does this improve the life of the person you're helping?
 (Ex: She enjoys the time we spend together.)

_____
_____
_____

SECTION III: ACTIVITY HANDOUTS

Becoming Dedicated

By changing your attitude, you can transform your actions and become dedicated to developing a lifestyle of helping others. How can you begin to shape your actions to become more dedicated to others?

For each person you mention, use a name code but not initials.

Needs of Other People	How I Can be More Helpful
(Ex: There are many hungry people in my community.)	(Ex: I will make a commitment to collect canned and boxed food from neighbors, once a month, and deliver the contributions to the local food kitchen.)

From Pain Comes Compassion

Most people have lived through some type of pain in their lives, and have grown from it. Self-pity can be replaced by compassion for others. Think about ways that you have experienced pain in your life and were able (or would like) to cultivate compassion.

For each person you mention, use a name code but not initials.

Pain in My Life	How I Turned (Or Could Turn) My Pain into Compassion
(Ex: I experienced depression after my parents separated.)	(Ex: I now volunteer to help others who are suffering with depression.)

SECTION III: ACTIVITY HANDOUTS

Being Kind

By simply being kind to other people, you can begin to cultivate generosity. Think about kind things you do, or could do, to begin to be more generous.

For each person you mention, use a name code but not initials.

List the people to whom are you **always** kind.
   (Ex: The cashiers at the stores, who are on their feet all day.)

_____
_____
_____
_____
_____
_____
_____

To whom are you **usually** kind?
   (Ex: MHK who is very nice but sometimes annoying.)

_____
_____
_____
_____
_____
_____

To whom are you **rarely** kind?
   (Ex: Our bus driver who is sometimes grouchy.)

_____
_____
_____
_____
_____
_____

(Continued on the next page)

SECTION III: ACTIVITY HANDOUTS

Being Kind (Continued)

To whom would you like to be **more kind**?
(Ex: The bus driver. I wouldn't want to be responsible for noisy kids.)

_____
_____
_____
_____
_____
_____

In what situations do you find it **hard to be kind** to others? Why?
(Ex: If someone's rude to others.)

_____
_____
_____
_____
_____
_____

When do you find it **easy to be kind** to others?
(Ex: When I can put myself in their shoes and understand.)

_____
_____
_____
_____
_____
_____

SECTION III: ACTIVITY HANDOUTS

Kindness

Who are five of the kindest people you know? How do they exhibit their kindness?

For each person you mention, use a name code but not initials.

1) _____

_____

_____

_____

_____

2) _____

_____

_____

_____

_____

3) _____

_____

_____

_____

_____

4) _____

_____

_____

_____

5) _____

_____

_____

_____

_____

SECTION III: JOURNALING ACTIVITIES

A Generosity Quotation

Real generosity is doing something nice for someone who will never find out.
                                                                ~ **Frank A. Clark**

Frank A. Clark's quote talks about random acts of kindness. Can you identify at least three ways you can help people this week without them knowing?

(Ex: *wipe up spilled water so nobody slips.*)

If you are mentioning a specific person use a name code but not initials.

_____
_____
_____
_____
_____
_____
_____
_____
_____
_____
_____
_____
_____
_____
_____
_____
_____
_____
_____
_____
_____
_____

If you and other participants are willing, share your list with each other. Be certain not to mention someone's name code if others might be able to identify it.

SECTION III: JOURNALING ACTIVITIES

Helping

In detail, journal about ways you help others with your time.

For each person you mention, use a name code but not initials.

_____
_____
_____
_____
_____
_____
_____
_____
_____
_____
_____
_____

How can you find time in your schedule to be of help to others?

_____
_____
_____
_____
_____
_____
_____
_____
_____
_____

(Continued on the next page)

SECTION III: JOURNALING ACTIVITIES

Helping *(Continued)*

Journal about the ways you can help anyone, with gifts, without spending a lot of money? Be creative.

For each person you mention, use a name code but not initials.

_____
_____
_____
_____
_____
_____
_____
_____
_____
_____
_____

Who can help you in the above projects?

_____
_____
_____
_____
_____
_____
_____
_____
_____
_____
_____

(Continued on the next page)

SECTION III: JOURNALING ACTIVITIES

Helping *(Continued)*

In what new ways would you like to begin helping others?

_____
_____
_____
_____
_____
_____
_____
_____

Write about what helping others can do for you?

_____
_____
_____
_____
_____
_____
_____
_____

What holds you back from helping others?

_____
_____
_____
_____
_____
_____
_____
_____

Facts about Generosity

- Generosity makes the helper feel good.

- Generosity reflects the intention of looking out for others.

- Generosity depletes feelings such as greed, jealousy and fear of loss.

- Generosity and helping others are spiritual acts.

- Generosity is the habit of giving freely without expecting anything in return.

- Generosity is offering time, gifts, money, talents, labor or resources to people in need.

- Generosity can happen at home, school, workplace, community – with friends, family or strangers – anywhere at anytime.

SECTION IV:
Kindness to the Global Community

Name_____

Date_____

SECTION IV: KINDNESS TO THE GLOBAL COMMUNITY SCALE

Kindness to the Global Community Scale Directions

The Kindness to the Global Community is designed to help you assess how kind you are to other people and to the global community. It will help you to explore your own lifestyle, as well as how you interact with nature, the environment and your local, national and global community,

This assessment contains 32 statements. Read each of the statements and decide if the statement is true or false for you. If it is true, circle the word TRUE next to the statement. If the statement is false, circle the word FALSE next to the statement. Ignore the letters after the True and False choices. They are for scoring purposes and will be used later.

In the following example, the circled True indicates that the item is true for the person completing the assessment:

1. I am involved in my community, parades, festivals or fairs . . . . . . (True (A))   False (B)

This is not a test and there are no right or wrong answers. Do not spend too much time thinking about your answers. Your initial response will likely be the most true for you. Be sure to respond to every statement.

(Turn to the next page and begin)

SECTION IV: KINDNESS TO THE GLOBAL COMMUNITY SCALE

Kindness to the Global Community Scale

1. I am involved in my community, parades, festivals or fairs. ...... True (A)   False (B)

2. I volunteer in my community. .... True (A)   False (B)

3. I spend more hours talking directly to people than
   browsing the Internet. .... True (A)   False (B)

4. I don't know the names of many of my neighbors. .... True (B)   False (A)

5. I know and/or trust the local police. .... True (A)   False (B)

6. I am not very sociable. .... True (B)   False (A)

7. I don't feel the need to make connections with people
   in my community. .... True (B)   False (A)

8. I believe I can make a difference in my community. .... True (A)   False (B)

                                                                 C TOTAL = _____

9. I encourage my family to conserve water. .... True (A)   False (B)

10. I will not wear hand-me-downs. .... True (B)   False (A)

11. I turn off electronics / lights to conserve energy. .... True (A)   False (B)

12. I prefer to ride a bicycle rather than ride a bus or travel in a car. ... True (A)   False (B)

13. I rarely walk anywhere. .... True (B)   False (A)

14. I arrange car pools with friends or friends' parents. ..... True (A)   False (B)

15. I would not use public transportation, even if available. . True (B)   False (A)

16. Conserving energy is not my problem. .... True (B)   False (A)

                                                                E TOTAL = _____

(Continued on the next page)

SECTION IV: KINDNESS TO THE GLOBAL COMMUNITY SCALE

(Kindness to the Global Community Scale continued)

17. I respect and value nature. . . . . True (A)   False (B)

18. I never litter outdoors. . . . . True (A)   False (B)

19. I understand the importance, as well as the beauty, of nature. . . . . True (A)   False (B)

20. I feel connected to nature and love to be outdoors. . . . . True (A)   False (B)

21. I think recycling takes too much time and effort. . . . . True (B)   False (A)

22. I feel it's my obligation to "keep green." . . . . True (A)   False (B)

23. I grow my own vegetables and/or fruit. . . . . True (A)   False (B)

24. I do not believe that conserving our environment is
    fundamental to our survival. . . . . True (B)   False (A)

N TOTAL = _____

25. I don't get enough exercise daily. . . . . True (B)   False (A)

26. I have a hard time balancing homework, chores,
    family, friends and play. . . . . True (B)   False (A)

27. I take my responsibilities seriously. . . . . True (A)   False (B)

28. I avoid potentially dangerous substances. . . . . True (B)   False (A)

29. I try to eat as many nutritional meals as possible. . . . . True (A)   False (B)

30. I work at managing my stress. . . . . True (A)   False (B)

31. I do not participate in any type of sports. . . . . True (B)   False (A)

32. I work at maintaining healthy relationships with my family. . . . . . . True (A)   False (B)

L TOTAL = _____

(Go to the Scoring Directions on the next page)

SECTION IV: KINDNESS TO THE GLOBAL COMMUNITY SCALE

Kindness to the Global Community Scale Scoring Directions

The Kindness to the Global Community Scale is designed to measure how kind you are to nature, the environment and to the global community in general.

To score the Kindness to the Global Community Scale:

Look at the 32 items you just completed. Focus on the "A" and "B" after each choice rather than the TRUE or FALSE. For each section, count the number of answers you circled with an "A" next to it. Put that number in the total blank at the end of each of the four sections. Transfer your scores to the lines below:

Section 1 TOTAL C = _____   **Community**

Section 2 TOTAL E = _____   **Energy**

Section 3 TOTAL N = _____   **Nature**

Section 4 TOTAL L = _____   **Kindness to Self Lifestyle**

Now, total all of your above scores to get your Grand Total.
Put that number on the line that follows:

Grand TOTAL   = _____

Turn to the next page to interpret your scores. You can interpret your scores for each of the individual scales, as well as your overall kindness to the global community.

SECTION IV: KINDNESS TO THE GLOBAL COMMUNITY SCALE

Kindness to the Global Community Scale Profile Interpretation

Total Scales Scores	Grand Total Scores	Result	Indications
6 to 8	**22 to 32**	high	You are very kind to the global community by conserving energy, recycling, protecting nature and living a wellness lifestyle. The following exercises you continue to display this kindness.
3 to 5	**11 to 21**	moderate	You are somewhat kind to the global community by conserving energy, recycling, protecting when possible and living a wellness lifestyle. The following exercises will help you further your kindness to the global community.
0 to 2	**0 to 10**	low	You can benefit from exploring ways to improve your attitude of being kind to the global community by conserving energy, recycling, and protecting nature and living a wellness lifestyle. The following exercises are designed to help you learn to be kind to the global community and to yourself.

The higher your score on the scales of this assessment, the kinder you are to the global community. In the areas in which you score in the **Moderate** or **Low** range, making an effort to improve on them will lead to feeling more spiritual. Whether you scored **Low**, **Moderate** or **High**, the exercises and activities that follow are designed to help you to begin, or continue on your path to helping make the global community a better place for future generations.

TEAM SUGGESTION FOR THE FACILITATOR:

After each teen completes the assessments individually, participants can be divided into four teams. One team can work on the Community activities, another on Energy, another on Nature and the last team on Kindness to Self Lifestyle activities. (pages 86 to 95) After each team completes their assigned pages, they take turns sharing their responses with the rest of the group and receive feedback. Team members may decide to implement their ideas in the real world!

SECTION IV: ACTIVITY HANDOUTS

Scale Description – Community

People scoring high on this scale are interested in one of the most critical aspects of being human – social bonding. They believe that much of the technology and busy-ness that we have in our lives actually isolates us from other people and the wellness benefits of social interaction. Think about your life. How socially interested are you?

MY SOCIAL NETWORK

People in My Life	Things I Do to Enhance My Social Interactions with Them
Family at Home	
Extended Family	
Good Friends	
School Friends	
Neighbors	
Spiritual / House of Worship	
Work / Volunteer	
Community	

(Continued on the next page)

SECTION IV: ACTIVITY HANDOUTS

MY PAST SOCIAL NETWORK

Many factors isolate us from other people. These isolations may be due to choices we make or from events that happen (moving to a new community, losing a job, etc.). What has happened that has kept you from being with other people?

People I No Longer See	Why?
Family at Home	
Extended Family	
Good Friends	
School Friends	
Neighbors	
Spiritual / House of Worship	
Work / Volunteer	
Community	

(Continued on the next page)

SECTION IV: ACTIVITY HANDOUTS

MY NETWORK

In what ways do you connect with friends in your community?
___
___
___
___

Are there volunteer opportunities in the community you might like to pursue?
___
___
___
___

How does where you live enhance the social connections you make?
___
___
___
___

How does where you live detract from the social connections you make?
___
___
___
___

How could you better connect with friends in your community, regardless of where you are living?
___
___
___
___

SECTION IV: ACTIVITY HANDOUTS

Scale Description – Energy

People scoring high on this scale are interested in energy conservation as a way to sustain the earth. They see our energy supply as a valuable commodity and they also believe that our global demand for energy is starting to exceed the supply. They believe that the energy shortage can be overcome to ensure that future generations have ample amounts of energy to use.

What are your thoughts about the energy problems in the global community?

_____
_____
_____
_____

How would you suggest we better preserve the energy sources we already have?

_____
_____
_____
_____

What public transportation resources exist in your community? How often do you use public transportation? Why or why not?

_____
_____
_____
_____

What changes can you make to your transportation needs to use less energy?

_____
_____
_____
_____

(Continued on the next page)

SECTION IV: ACTIVITY HANDOUTS

CONSERVING ENERGY

What can you suggest to your family to conserve energy?

_____
_____
_____

How can you personally conserve energy more effectively?

_____
_____
_____

Go onto the Internet and research some of the energy-saving websites. List the websites you found below and the information you found interesting. Share the websites.

Website	Information

Scale Description – Nature

People scoring high on this scale enjoy being part of nature and spending time in natural surroundings. They believe that preserving nature is critical for human survival, and will do what they can to ensure that the natural environment will be preserved for future generations. They feel connected to nature and spend as much time in nature as possible.

What do you like about our natural world?

_____
_____
_____

What can you do to preserve this natural world?

_____
_____
_____

How do you spend time with nature?

_____
_____
_____

What prevents you from spending more time in a natural setting?

_____
_____
_____

How can you change that?

_____
_____
_____

(Continued on the next page)

SECTION IV: ACTIVITY HANDOUTS

Preserving Nature

What types of things can you begin doing to help preserve the natural environment? In the table that follows, list the things you personally will begin doing to make sure that the natural environment survives to be enjoyed by future generations.

Aspects of Nature Preservation	What I Can Begin Doing
Gardening	
Recycling	
Developing and/or Attending Environmental Programs	
Plant Trees	
Assist Animals	
Spend Time Enjoying Nature	
Other	
Other	

SECTION IV: ACTIVITY HANDOUTS

Scale Description – Kindness-to-Self Lifestyle

People scoring high on this scale are interested in living more simply and more consciously. They are interested in living as stress-free as possible, and they are not interested in comparing themselves to others and keeping up with their friends. They define success on their own terms and live a lifestyle based on that definition.

What do you do to reduce the stress in your life?

_____
_____
_____
_____

How can you be a more responsible person?

_____
_____
_____
_____

What can you do to begin eating healthier?

_____
_____
_____
_____

Create a plan to increase your exercise.

_____
_____
_____
_____

(Continued on the next page)

DEFINING SUCCESS

Success can be very difficult to define. Many people think that to live a successful life they have to make a lot of money and have a lot of "toys." People, however, are beginning to redefine their notions of success.

How do you define success?

_____
_____
_____

In the various roles that you play, list below what you *currently* consider successful?

Roles I Play	How I Measure Success
Family Member	
Student	
Friend	
Worker	
Neighbor / Community Resident	
Other	

(Continued on the next page)

SECTION IV: ACTIVITY HANDOUTS

REDEFINING SUCCESS

In the various roles that you play, what would you consider successful if you were being kinder to the global community?

Roles I Play	How I Measure Success
Family Member	
Student	
Friend	
Worker	
Neighbor / Community Resident	
Other	

What changes will you need to make to redefine success for you?

_____
_____
_____
_____

SECTION IV: JOURNALING ACTIVITIES

Kindness-to-the-Global Community Quotations

Put check marks by the quotes that you feel would inspire you to greater heights of life satisfaction. You can cut the quotes out, post them by your computer or on your refrigerator or tuck one in your wallet. At the bottom of the page, write about why those particular quotes speak to you.

☐ *To me a lush carpet of pine needles or spongy grass is more welcome than the most luxurious Persian rug.* ~ **Helen Keller**

☐ *Our survival depends on the healing power of love, intimacy and relationships. As individuals. As communities. As a country. As a culture. Perhaps even as a species.* ~ **Dean Ornish**

☐ *The cheapest energy is the energy you don't use in the first place.* ~ **Sheryl Crow**

☐ *The more you extend kindness to yourself, the more it will become your natural response to others.* ~ **Wayne Dyer**

_____
_____
_____
_____
_____
_____
_____
_____
_____
_____
_____
_____
_____
_____
_____

Preserving the Global Community

Why is preserving the global community important?

_____

_____

_____

_____

_____

_____

_____

_____

_____

_____

_____

_____

What will you do to be kind to the global community?

_____

_____

_____

_____

_____

_____

_____

_____

_____

_____

_____

_____

Be Kind to the Global Community

- Grow your own fruits and vegetables
- Keep apprised of environmental issues
- Purchase gently used items
- Recycle
- Reduce your amount of energy
- Spend more time with family and friends, and less on consumption
- Start a "Save a Can" or "Save a Plastic Bag" campaign in your neighborhood or school
- Think "GREEN"
- Act "GREEN"
- Use public transportation when possible
- Write to your congress people about environmental issues that are important to you and your global community

Kind People . . .

- are kind to themselves
- do not expect anything in return
- are pleasant, tender, compassionate and caring
- pay it forward
- feel responsible for the welfare of others
- care about the greater good of humanity
- show empathy for others
- receive joy from helping others
- are unselfish
- are benevolent

SECTION V:
Teen Social Action Scale

Name_____

Date_____

SECTION V: SOCIAL ACTION SCALE

Social Action Scale Directions

Social Action is the intentional personal and/or community action to organize for social change. These changes can involve the following interests:

- Political/governmental actions
- Economic changes
- Environmental improvements
- Racial equality
- Cultural acceptance
- Humane and animal rights
- Social justice
- Feeding and clothing people in need

The Social Action Scale is designed to help you identify your involvement and / or desire to be a social activist in your local, national or global community. When referring to community, it can be your immediate neighborhood, your religious or spiritual community, a school club, an organization, etc.

This scale contains 40 statements divided into four scales. Read each of the statements and decide whether or not the statement describes you. If the statement describes you, circle the **YES** next to the statement. If it does not describe you, circle the **NO** next to the statement.

In the following example, the circled YES indicates the statement is descriptive of the person completing the inventory.

I easily connect with other people . . . . (YES)   NO

This is not a test and there are no right or wrong answers. Do not spend too much time thinking about your answers. Your initial response will likely be the most true for you. Be sure to respond to every statement.

(Turn to the next page and begin)

SECTION V: SOCIAL ACTION SCALE

Social Action Scale

I easily connect with other people	YES	NO
I do not see other people as inferior to me	YES	NO
Everyone has a right to personal opinions	YES	NO
I believe that people are inherently good	YES	NO
I feel morally obligated to help others	YES	NO
I am not self-centered	YES	NO
I love others as much as I love myself	YES	NO
I find the good in people	YES	NO
If others thrive, I feel as if I thrive as well	YES	NO
All people are worth helping	YES	NO

P - TOTAL = _____

I value relationships more than money	YES	NO
I like to volunteer my time and energy	YES	NO
I help others because I like it, not out of a sense of obligation	YES	NO
I don't mind giving up computer time to be a volunteer	YES	NO
I do not expect anything in return for helping others	YES	NO
I will make sacrifices for the welfare of others	YES	NO
I am motivated to help other people	YES	NO
I do not help others in order to be acknowledged	YES	NO
Helping others enriches my inner-self	YES	NO
I care, and want to help people less fortunate that I am	YES	NO

W - TOTAL = _____

(Continued on the next page)

SECTION V: SOCIAL ACTION SCALE

(Social Action Scale continued)

I have a great desire to help others.	YES	NO
I want to make my community better.	YES	NO
I like to get involved in community affairs	YES	NO
I enjoy volunteering	YES	NO
I do what I can to be a part of my community	YES	NO
I obey the laws and rules of society	YES	NO
I strive to be environmentally "green".	YES	NO
I am a good neighbor	YES	NO
I relate well to others in my community	YES	NO
I am tolerant of others' differences	YES	NO

C - TOTAL = _____

I like to be with other people	YES	NO
I speak up when I see wrongs and injustices	YES	NO
I like to support a good cause.	YES	NO
I assume personal responsibility for public problems.	YES	NO
I am able to develop and maintain supportive relationships.	YES	NO
I can be counted on in times of need	YES	NO
I treat other people who are like me, or different from me, with respect and fairness	YES	NO
I like being part of a team.	YES	NO
I assume personal responsibility for public problems	YES	NO
I want to make the world a better place for future generations	YES	NO

S - TOTAL = _____

(Go to the Scoring Directions on the next page)

SECTION V: SOCIAL ACTION SCALE

Social Action Scale
Scoring Directions

This assessment is designed to measure your present and potential interest in social activism. For each of the four sections, count the number of YES answers you circled. Put that total on the line marked TOTAL at the end of each section.

Transfer your totals to the spaces below:

      P   Positive View of Others TOTAL = _____

      W The Welfare of Others   TOTAL = _____

      C   Sense of Community   TOTAL = _____

      S   Social Support   TOTAL = _____

Now, add your four scores together to get your Social Action Scale Grand Total.

                Grand Total – Social Action Scale = _____

Profile Interpretation

Total Scale Scores	Grand Total Scale Scores	Result	Indications
7 to 10	27 to 40	high	You show a great deal of interest in social action. The following exercises will help you continue your social activism.
4 to 6	14 to 26	moderate	You show some interest in social action. The following exercises will help promote your social activism.
0 to 3	0 to 13	low	At this point social action is not of interest to you right now. The following exercises will help you explore potential areas of social activism.

Start with scales on which you scored in the **Moderate** or **High** range. Find the descriptions on the pages that follow. Read the descriptions and complete the exercises that are included. No matter how you scored, low, moderate or high, you will benefit from these exercises.

SECTION V: SOCIAL ACTION SCALE

Social Action Scale Descriptions

Positive View of Others

People scoring high on this scale feel connected to other human beings. They believe that people are inherently good and worthy of all of the help they need. They are able to develop connections with others, are trustworthy and loyal to both their family and others. They make new friends easily and treat all people fairly and with respect.

The Welfare of Others

People scoring high on this scale are truly concerned about the welfare of other human beings. They relate well with others, care about others less fortunate than themselves and are able to put themselves in the shoes of others to better understand their world. They are respectful and tolerant of others who may be different from them. They are willing to volunteer their time and energy to help others and make the world a better place.

Sense of Community

People scoring high on this scale feel a sense of community with other human beings. They are "people-people" who are able to develop the spirit of teamwork and cooperation with those around them. They rarely view others with jealousy or suspicion. They do not attempt to outdo others or put them down. They enjoy mutual support and work together to accomplish mutual goals. They love themselves but do not have a self-centered view of themselves. They enjoy reaching out and being with other people.

Social Support

People scoring high on this scale can be counted on by all human beings in times of need. They are friendly, concerned about others, and caring. They are interested in other people, in humanity in general and in the environment. They are cooperative, non-competitive and treat all people well regardless of who they are. They are tolerant of differences and treat all people with respect.

Reflecting on Your Social Altruism

Social action is being involved and interested in helping in any way, alone or along with other people. It is trying to make the world a better place.

When people are socially active, they are driven by a pure heart and have no other personal motives or agendas. They are activists because they feel there is a cause worth fighting for, and they go about it in an organized manner with other people who feel the same.

Motives

Do you have a particular cause you would like to work on? *(Ex: Help organize a teen Breast Cancer Team)*

_____
_____
_____
_____

What is your motivation? *(Ex: My aunt had breast cancer)*

_____
_____
_____
_____

How will society be better for the service you provide? *(Ex: My contribution will raise money for research)*

_____
_____
_____
_____

How will doing this help you connect with other people? *(Ex: I will meet like-minded people)*

_____
_____
_____
_____

SECTION V: ACTIVITY HANDOUTS

Interests

By exploring your interests, you will be better able to explore the types of activism you would like to provide.

What do you enjoy doing? Can you incorporate any of these into an activism action?
_____
_____
_____
_____
_____
_____

About what do you have a passion - politics, a disease, economics, racism, animal rights, etc.?
_____
_____
_____
_____
_____
_____

Do any of those passions you listed have a social action group? If not, how can you start one?
_____
_____
_____
_____
_____
_____

What injustices or problems do you see that you would like to help repair?
_____
_____
_____
_____
_____
_____

SECTION V: ACTIVITY HANDOUTS

My Volunteering – Small Projects

Social activism does not need to be restricted to large-scale helping projects like charity marathons. In actuality, there are many different ways of helping, including small projects like picking up litter in your community or helping push a stalled car out of the street. In the following table, think about some of the small things you have volunteered to do to be helpful.

Places I Have Volunteered	How I Have Volunteered
Community	
Neighborhood	
Region	
School	
House of Worship / Spiritual	
Others	

SECTION V: ACTIVITY HANDOUTS

My Volunteering – Large Projects

Social Activism can also include large-scale helping projects like starting a charity march, beginning a recycle campaign, organizing a Thanksgiving dinner for people in need, helping build houses for people, or helping with homeless children. In the following table, think about some of the major things you have done or are now doing to serve others.

Places I Have Volunteered	How I Have Volunteered
Community	
Neighborhood	
Region	
School	
House of Worship / Spiritual	
Others	

SECTION V: ACTIVITY HANDOUTS

Where or How I Can Help

It is important that you consider the areas where you think that you can help the most. Identification of these areas will be based on your interests and skills, and what you believe are the critical areas to fill needs. Volunteering to help as a teenager can lead to great activism in the future.

What needs are present that you would like to fill?

Areas that Might Need My Helping Skills	Where and How I Can Help
Volunteer at a Animal Shelter	
Read to the elderly	
Babysit with children for working parents	
Prepare and serve in a food kitchen	
Tutor English to a new foreign student	
Participate with Earth Day	
Respond to a natural disaster	

(Continued on the next page)

SECTION V: ACTIVITY HANDOUTS

Where or How I Can Help *(Continued)*

Areas that Might Need My Helping Skills	Where and How I Can Help
Clean up parks and / or beaches	
Pick up litter in the neighborhood	
Help with Habitat for Humanity	
Deliver or prepare Meals on Wheels	
Address postcards for political campaigns	
Put away books at the library	
Volunteer to do office work at an agency	
Collect recycling items	
Sort cans at a food bank	

(Continued on the next page)

SECTION V: ACTIVITY HANDOUTS

Where or How I Can Help *(Continued)*

Areas that Might Need My Helping Skills	Where and How I Can Help
Help at a Neighborhood Watch	
Help at the school office	
Be a docent at the zoo or museum	
Volunteer at a drug rehab center	
Investigate the needs of a civic club	
Try a community theater	
Volunteer at a day care center	
Offer to regularly sweep the sidewalk for an aged neighbor	
Collect and donate used clothing	

(Continued on the next page)

SECTION V: ACTIVITY HANDOUTS

Where or How I Can Help *(Continued)*

Areas that Might Need My Helping Skills	Where and How I Can Help
Think about an exchange student	
Volunteer to be a runner at a hospital	
Help with Special Olympics	
Have a garage sale and donate money	
Cook at a homeless shelter	
Start a singing group or band and perform at assisted living facilities	
Other	
Other	
Other	

SECTION V: ACTIVITY HANDOUTS

Benefits of Volunteering

There are many benefits of being a volunteer to both the people whom you serve, as well as to yourself. Think about how the help you have provided in the past has been of benefit to you, or how the help you are interested in providing in the future can benefit you.

Ways Volunteering Can Benefit People	How Volunteering Has Benefitted You
Learn New Skills	
Provide Meaning	
Reduce Stress	
Provide Sense of Satisfaction	
Broaden Experiences	
Enrich Life	
Contribute Toward Career Development	

SECTION V: ACTIVITY HANDOUTS

Why Not?

If you have not helped others in the past, respond below.

Reasons I have not helped or volunteered in the past:

1. _____
2. _____
3. _____

What are your thoughts about volunteering after doing the activities in this book?

_____
_____
_____
_____

What is your reluctance about volunteering?

_____
_____
_____
_____

What positive messages have you received about volunteering or social activism?

_____
_____
_____
_____

What negative messages have you received about volunteering or social activism?

_____
_____
_____
_____

© 2011 WHOLE PERSON ASSOCIATES, 210 WEST MICHIGAN ST., DULUTH MN 55802-1908 • 800-247-6789

SECTION V: JOURNALING ACTIVITIES

Do Good Anyway

The verse below was written on the wall of Mother Teresa's home for children in Calcutta, India, and is widely attributed to her.

People are unreasonable, illogical, and self-centered. Love them anyway. If you are good, people may accuse you of selfish motives. Do good anyway. If you are successful, you may win false friends and true enemies. Succeed anyway. The good you do today may be forgotten tomorrow. Do good anyway. Honesty and transparency make you vulnerable. Be honest and transparent anyway. What you spend years building may be destroyed overnight. Build anyway. People who really want to help may attack you if you help them. Help them anyway. Give the world the best you have and you may get hurt. Give the world your best anyway.

How can you apply this quote to your daily life?

_____
_____
_____
_____
_____
_____
_____
_____
_____
_____
_____
_____
_____
_____
_____
_____
_____
_____

SECTION V: JOURNALING ACTIVITIES

Being a Volunteer and/or Social Activist

What about being a social activist or volunteer appeals to you?

_____
_____
_____
_____
_____
_____

What will you begin?

_____
_____
_____

When?

_____
_____
_____

Where?

_____
_____
_____

How?

_____
_____
_____

Why?

_____
_____
_____

Excuses People Use to Avoid Helping Others

- *"I will feel silly and embarrassed."*

- *"I will look silly."*

- *"There are no opportunities to help others."*

- *"I can't make a difference by myself."*

- *"I will look like a goody two-shoes."*

- *"I'm not very civic-minded."*

- *"My friends would ridicule me."*

- *"It's not my responsibility."*

- *"People don't appreciate my help."*

- *"The government should do something about it."*

- *"I don't have time."*

Don't let these messages keep you from helping others!

SECTION V: EDUCATIONAL HANDOUTS

Tips for Your Volunteer Experiences

- **Identify volunteer opportunities of interest to you.**

- **Volunteer on a consistent basis. (even if it is one hour a week or month)**

- **Start slowly — don't over-extend yourself.**

- **Prepare for negative, as well as positive, experiences.**

- **Ask for training if you need it.**

- **Gather as much information as possible about the volunteer site.**

- **Don't expect anything in return for your service.**

- **Research the cause and/or facility.**

- **Consider the skills you have to offer.**

- **Invite family and friends to join you.**

- **Keep your sense of humor.**

- **Bring your warm heart.**

Whole Person Associates is the leading publisher of training resources for professionals who empower people to create and maintain healthy lifestyles. Our creative resources will help you work effectively with your clients in the areas of stress management, wellness promotion, mental health and life skills.

Please visit us at our web site: www.wholeperson.com. You can check out our entire line of products, place an order, request our print catalog, and sign up for our monthly special notifications.

Whole Person Associates
210 W Michigan
Duluth MN 55802
800-247-6789